Amgueddfa Genedlaethol Cymru
National Museum of Wales
Cardiff 1982

Welsh History through Seals

This book was written by the
Reverend Dr. David H. Williams, F.S.A.

Department of Archaeology and Numismatics

Acknowledgements

The Department of Archaeology and Numismatics, and the author in particular, wish to thank all those involved in the preparation of this booklet, especially the Museum photographer Mr. Eric Broadbent and his colleagues for much fine work, and Mr. J. M. Lewis for many helpful suggestions. Many other individuals and corporate bodies have also contributed to the wide range of this little work.

The following persons and authorities have kindly given their permission for the reproduction of seals:

The British Library (17, 34, 38, 43-5, 52-4, 60, 63, 69, 70, 72, 74)
The British Museum (3, 5)
The National Library of Wales (65, 75)
The Public Record Office (25, 39, 49, 58, 64, 68, 76, 77, 87)
The Society of Antiquaries (2)
The Principal, St. David's University College, Lampeter (102)
The Principal, University College of North Wales, Bangor (30, 48)
The Archives Nationales, Paris (1, 46)
The Dean and Chapter, Canterbury Cathedral (67)
The Dean and Chapter, Hereford Cathedral (35, 57, 66, 73)
The Dean and Chapter, St. Asaph Cathedral (Cover illustration and 106)
Clwyd Record Office (20)
Dyfed Archive Service (103)
Glamorgan Archive Service (88, 93)
Gwynedd Record Office (42)
Carmarthen County Museum (95)
Monmouth Museum, Monmouth District Museums Service (56)
Newport Museum (81)
National Railway Museum, Swindon (83-86)
National Railway Museum, York (82: Crown Copyright)
Powysland Museum (99)
The Town Clerk, Haverfordwest (8)
Powys County Council (97)
Lloyds Bank Ltd. (96)
National Coal Board (78-79)
The Warden of Ruthin (101)
The Worshipful Company of Haberdashers (100)
The Earl of Cawdor (71)
Gabb and Sons, Solicitors, Abergavenny (80)
C. Gordon-Lloyd, Esq., (18)
Lt.Col. J.C.E. Harding-Rolls (24)
C. Methuen-Campbell, Esq., (10, 11, 16, 26-29, 32, 33, 40, 51, 59)
A.D.H. Pennant, Esq., (31)
E. A. Roberts, Esq., (22)
Dr. Michael Siddons (47)
Colbourne, Colman and Lawrence, Solicitors, (94)
Sir Owen Watkin Williams-Wynn (36, 37)

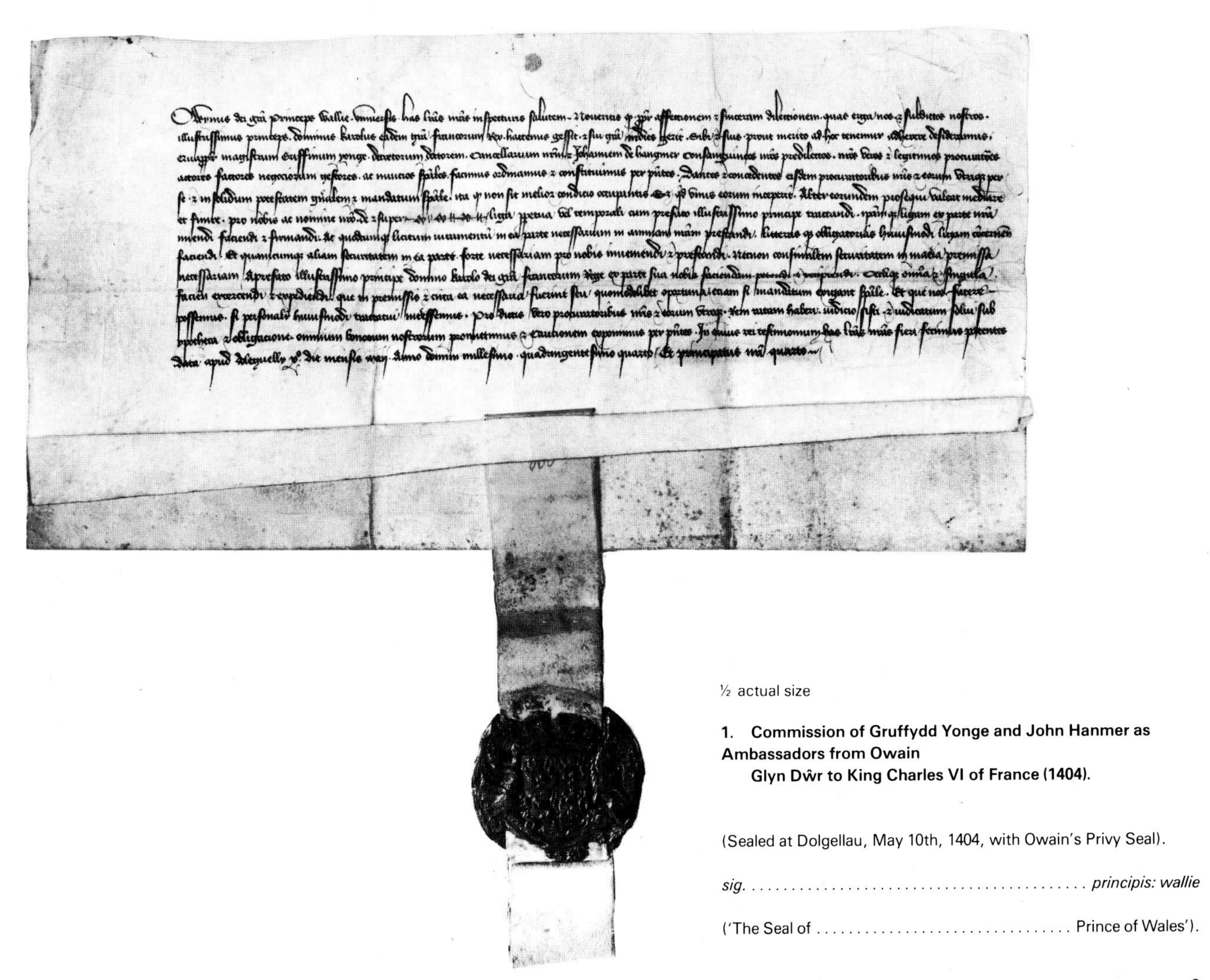

½ actual size

1. Commission of Gruffydd Yonge and John Hanmer as Ambassadors from Owain Glyn Dŵr to King Charles VI of France (1404).

(Sealed at Dolgellau, May 10th, 1404, with Owain's Privy Seal).

sig. .... principis: wallie

('The Seal of .... Prince of Wales').

Introduction

"Jezebel wrote letters in Ahab's name, and sealed them with his seal".
(1 Kings 21/8: *c.850 B.C.)*

From the earliest days of man's ability to communicate his thoughts in the written word and to set down his personal, business and legal transactions in formal documents, there has been a need for a mechanism which could both keep such writings and deeds secret and be able to assure the recipient and interested parties of their authenticity. This was especially important in an age of slow communications, when there could be no quick and ready contact between individuals, and when the handwriting might very often be that of a scribe, not of the sender.

The *seal* has fulfilled this two-fold purpose from antiquity: (i) to *authenticate* documents meant for public inspection and therefore left open, 'letters patent'; (ii) to *close* deeds and letters in order to keep their contents private. Most of the Welsh seals described in this booklet were used with the first purpose in mind – to help prove rights of title to the current and later generations. Distinction must be made between the seal proper (the *matrix* or *die*) and the image gained from it (the *impression* or *sealing*) by applying the matrix to softened bees-wax.

The earliest known Welsh seals date from the late twelfth century, and throughout the centuries of the Middle Ages which followed great importance continued to be attached to the sealing of documents. Charters and other deeds were of little or no value unless a distinctive seal-impression was attached. All persons of importance had their own proper seal of recognisable design and legend; and bodies corporate, similarly, their 'common seal'. Lesser individuals frequently had the seal of a superior person, perhaps the local lord, applied to documents recording important business.

Important transactions might bear the seals of several adjudicators and witnesses. A deed of release in 1272 by prince Rhodri in favour of his brother, Llywelyn ap Gruffydd, was sealed "for greater security" with the seals of the bishops of Bangor and St. Asaph, the abbots of Aberconwy, Basingwerk and Enlli, and the archdeacons of Bangor and St. Asaph. The significance of the seal continued into modern times, for a corporate body could not transact business without a common seal. Thus the statutes of Friars School, Bangor, directed the trustees to obtain a common seal (1568), as did the letters patent of Elizabeth I (1576) in respect of the Warden and Governors of the 'Free Grammar School, Carmarthen'. When St. David's College, Lampeter, had been founded (1828), several ecclesiastical livings were placed in its gift, but the College found that it could not legally take possession of these without a common seal, which was, therefore, prepared. Even today a conventional 'seal' is applied to personal legal documents.

The importance attached to seals is illustrated by the suspicion shown to a bull of Honorius IV approving the transference of Cistercian monks in North Wales from Aberconwy to Maenan (1284). Honorius issued his decree in the interval between his election and consecration in 1285; the attached seal impression raised doubts as to the document's authenticity, and, at Edward I's request, his successor, Nicholas IV, confirmed his predecessor's decree, and found it necessary to state that "papal bulls issued before their consecration bear no name on the lead seal, which has given rise to a popular error that such bulls are defective." In similar vein, the abbot of Neath in 1336, requesting Edward III to confirm the charter granted to his monastery by King John in 1207, noted that the charter had been "so much ruined and worn by the wars in South Wales", that "the seal is in part broken, but is recognisable enough." This underlines the need felt for a seal to be distinctive, 'peculiar' or especial, proper to that person or body alone.

Quite commonly, in the Middle Ages and later, seals might be stolen and fraudulently used. In a monastic dispute about 1442 abbot Rhys of Strata Florida came to Cymer Abbey in Meirionydd, evicted its abbot, John Cobbe, took the monastery's common seal, and used it to make grants and leases, probably favourable to his friends. Such instances were not uncommon. Care was therefore taken to ensure the safe custody and proper use of seals by their owners, be they individuals or corporations. The keeping of the seal in a bag (to prevent physical wear and tear), or in a locked chest (to inhibit theft), were frequent precautionary measures. Destruction or defacement of the seal-matrix on the death of its owner was commonly practised, and explains the relative rarity of matrices to-day.

The seals associated with the spread of royal authority in Wales had official *keepers,* appointed to ensure the proper custody of the seal, and sometimes a *cursitor*, whose job it was to impress the seal as required. To guard against fraudulent use, the Court of Aldermen at Cardiff ordered in 1819 that the Corporation Seal was not to be affixed to any deed or document "unless at a Court of Common Council." It is not surprising to find, in view of such precautions, that seals were sometimes forged. Indeed, it was alleged of the last abbot of Strata Florida that after the suppression of his abbey (1539) he issued a lease of a grange" by writing under a counterfeit seal, like the convent seal of the monastery."

The matrices of Welsh seals have sometimes been found in unexpected places: one of Tintern was discovered in the moat of Ewenny Priory, that of the Guild of the Holy Trinity, Cardiff, was found in a heap of manure in a turnip field, that of the Chancery of Monmouth was located in the bed of the river Wye and later used as the bob of a clock-pendulum; further afield, the matrix of the Collegiate Church at Abergwili was found in spoil turned up during the excavation of the M1 motorway in Leicestershire. Similarly, the seal of Kelso Abbey in Scotland was found in a Carmarthenshire garden.

The collections of the National Museum include an interesting group of fourteen leaden papal bullae. These include those of Honorius III (1216-27) and of Gregory IX (1370-8) found during excavations at Cwmhir and Strata Florida Abbeys. Other such bullae have been discovered at Cymer, Margam and Tintern Abbeys, whilst more recently (1979) a lead bulla of Benedict XII (1335-42) has been found at the site of Carmarthen Priory.

In several instances, Welsh seal-impressions have found their way, with the documents to which they were attached, out of Wales, and many now repose in the Public Record Office and elsewhere. The study of Welsh seals to-day still owes much to the work of Victorian sigillographers who made collections of copies or casts of Welsh seals. Two men of note in this respect were George Grant Francis, FSA, the Cambrians' Local Secretary for Glamorgan, who wrote in 1858 that he proposed to bring together "impressions of all the known *Welsh seals,* fix them on proper mounts, and place them for public sight" in the Royal Institution of South Wales in Swansea. In the following year, it could be reported that the collection of "seals connected with Wales", formed by Robert Ready and executed in gutta-percha, comprised 271 specimens. Copies of the collection were in the Swansea and Carmarthen Museums, and a set could be purchased for 6 guineas.

As this booklet seeks to show, the use of seals was by no means confined to the Middle Ages, but continued to be of significance into the twentieth century. Their use in Wales, from the late twelfth century onwards, by corporate bodies of very different functions, and by innumerable individuals both ecclesiastical and secular, make them a veritable "mirror of history". The seals depicted here are meant also to be representative of the whole of Wales, and indeed of the several repositories, in Wales and beyond, where Welsh seals are now preserved. Wherever possible, the seals illustrated are original impressions rather than modern casts, and unless stated to the contrary they are reproduced at their actual size.

The Process of Sealing: The Matrix or Die

Matrices were commonly manufactured in copper alloys – brass, bronze or latten. Silver might be employed by people of higher rank and by wealthier institutions, lead by poorer people. The matrix was the work of a skilled engraver. Sometimes matrices were non-metallic, formed from stone or slate. Similarities of design and legend amongst certain Welsh seals, suggest common sources.

Both the matrices shown on this page have been altered:
(1) the brass seal-die of Grace Dieu Abbey by the addition of *Et Conventus,* 'and the convent', probably in the early fourteenth century after papal and royal injunctions commanding Cistercian monasteries to have a common seal;
(2) the silver seal-die of Strata Florida Abbey by the defacement of the name of the abbot, probably on his death, in order to economise by not having a completely new seal engraved.

2. Grace Dieu Abbey (13th-14th Century)

SIGILLVM: ABBATIS:
ET CONVENT' DE GRACIA DEI
(The Seal of the Abbot and the Convent of Grace Dieu)

(Matrix)

(Impression)

(Reverse of matrix)

3. Strata Florida Abbey (15th Century)

Sigill' . . . abb'is de strata florida
(The Seal of . . . ., abbot of Strata Florida).
The reverse of the matrix generally had a hinge or ridge for handling the seal, often pierced with a hole for attaching and securing it by a lace or thong.

4. Rural Dean of Llŷn
(Early 13th Century)

\+ *SIGILL ENNII DECANI DE LEIN*
(The Seal of Einon, dean of Llŷn)
A slate matrix found at Mynydd Ednyfed, near Criccieth, about 1890. It bears a fish, possibly the heraldic 'luce' or pike.

5. Borough of Criccieth
(Late 13th Century)

\+ *S': COMVNE DE CRVKIN IN WAL'*
(The Common Seal of Criccieth in Wales)
A latten matrix found at Trawsfynydd about 1900. It probably dates from the establishment of the borough of Criccieth in 1284 by Edward I. A triple towered castle is shown within a curtain wall. On the left-hand tower a man sits blowing a horn, his feet dangling; on the right a dragon, with the floriated tail characteristic of this period.

6. Hywel ap William (14th Century)

\+ *S': HOWELI : AP : WILLT̄*
(The Seal of Hywel ap William)
A stone matrix perforated possibly for a handle. Found at Llangynllo, Powys, in 1966.

7. Fraternity of the Trinity, Cardiff
(15th Century)

S . fris̄ . trinitatis . de . Kardif . in galis
(The Seal of the Fraternity of the Trinity of Cardiff in Wales).
The brass matrix, displaying the Holy Trinity, of a medieval guild.

The Process of Sealing: Impressing

⅔ actual size

⅔ actual size

8. Haverfordwest Town Seal
(obverse)
+ *SIGILLUM : COMVNE : DE : HAWERFORDIA*
(The Common Seal of Haverford)
(reverse)
+ *O LECTOR : SALVE : CELI : PATEANT : TIBI : UALVE*
(Hail! O Reader, may the gates of heaven open wide for you).

This common seal probably dates from about 1291, when Edward I gave their Charter to the burgesses of Haverford. The obverse depicts a single-masted ship with fore-stay, back-stay, shrouds and halliards, a clinker-built hull, a side rudder, and embattled fore-, after-, and top-castles from which bowmen could shoot down upon the decks of an enemy ship. In the fore-castle a mariner is blowing a horn, in the after-castle another is sounding a trumpet. The counter-seal shows a castle with gate-house; on the tower a man is blowing a trumpet; underneath is a wyvern (a two-legged dragon) with a lion rampant to the left and a perched eagle to the right.

⅔ actual size

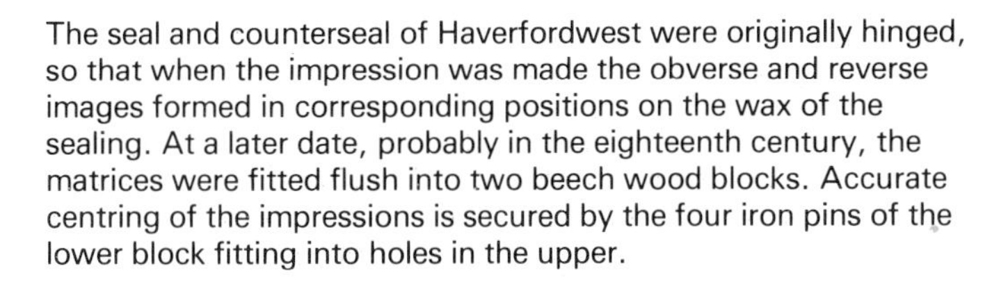

The seal and counterseal of Haverfordwest were originally hinged, so that when the impression was made the obverse and reverse images formed in corresponding positions on the wax of the sealing. At a later date, probably in the eighteenth century, the matrices were fitted flush into two beech wood blocks. Accurate centring of the impressions is secured by the four iron pins of the lower block fitting into holes in the upper.

9. Chancery of Monmouth

The brass matrix of the Chancery of Monmouth, dating from the reign of Edward IV (1461-83), still exhibits one of the original four perforated ears to fit the counter-seal. It is a typical equestrian seal, with the arms of England displayed on the shield and the caparisons of the horse.

S : Edwardi : dei : gra : reg : Angl : t : Francie : cancellarie : sue : de : Monemouth̄
(The seal of Edward, by the grace of God King of England and France, in his chancery of Monmouth).

Affixing The Seal

It was extremely important to affix a seal to a document in such a way that it could not be easily removed. This was done either (i) by making incisions in the fold of the document and passing a strip of parchment or a length of woven cord, often of silk, through them, the seal being impressed over the ends (**Plate 10**) or (ii) by cutting a strip of the parchment from the lower edge of the manuscript, and impressing the seal upon it. (**Plate 11**).

10. Gilbert de Clare, lord of Glamorgan (C.1220)

(For the reverse of this seal see **Plate 40**)

11. John Gruffydd, Abbot of Margam (1527)

(counter-seal)

The Seal: Design and Colour

Each seal impression so affixed to a document possessed five attributes which helped to give the individual seal its distinctive character, and which assist in its classification and identification should it have become detached. These physical properties of each impressed seal were its size, shape, device or motif, colour and legend.

Medieval seals varied in *size,* the larger ones indicating the greater dignity and status of their owners. The *shape* was almost invariably round or oval. *Round* seals were used by civic bodies and by laymen of all ranks, *oval* seals by ecclesiastics and ladies; but there were numerous exceptions to these two generalisations. *Pointed oval* seals became common from the thirteenth century onwards. Most seals bore a *motif* or *device.* Whilst a variety of miscellaneous devices was employed by lesser folk, nobles and knights usually had on the obverse of sealing an *equestrian* figure representing the owner on horseback, and on the reverse, the *armorial* bearings proper to him. The greater the elaboration of detail, the later in date the seal is likely to be. A *lady* of note was often depicted in hunting costume, or else bearing two shields – one with the arms of her husband, the other displaying those of her father.

Sealing was largely accomplished with bees-wax, very often *coloured* by pigments such as orpiment (for yellow), vermilion (for red), verdigris (for green), or organic matter (for brown). No hard and fast rules can be determined regarding the choice of colours, but in general royal seals used *green* for important charters, *brown* for less significant documents, and *red* for privy seals and signets. Green was widely in use from the late twelfth century onwards, red from the early thirteenth.

The Legend

The evolving styles of lettering employed on medieval seals are well exemplified in Wales. Roman capitals are used until about 1200, Lombardic script to around 1350, then Black Letter down to the early 16th Century, with Renaissance Capitals appearing in the later Tudor period. The lettering employed on a loose sealing can be a useful aid in dating it. The differing styles can be exemplified by observing the form taken by the word *sigillum* (seal), or its contractions, *sigill'* and *sigillū.*

12. Roman Capitals
Seal of Milo of Gloucester (1140-43).

13. Lombardic Script
Seal of Henry, Bishop of Llandaff (1193-1218).

14. Black Letter
Seal of Thomas, Bishop of Llandaff (1398-1407).

15. Renaissance Capitals
Seal for Arwystli Deanery (c.1549-).

Motifs and Devices

Armorial and Equestrian

Several typical equestrian seals appear elsewhere in this booklet, but that of Morgan Gam is unusual in that it is pointed oval, equestrian seals generally being round in shape.

16. Morgan Gam, lord of Afan (c.1230)

+ SIGILLVM . MORGANI . CAM
(The Seal of Morgan Gam)

17. John Charlton, lord of Powys (1368)

**Sigillu:ioh'is:de:cherleton- e: dn̄i:powisie*
(The Seal of John de Charlton, lord of Powys).

18. Thomas Kemeys, Lord of Caerwent (1463)

19. Ithel ap Bleddyn (? Escheator of Flint) (c.1350)

Sigillu:Ithel:ap:Bledyn
(The Seal of Ithel ap Bleddyn)

20. Exchequer of Holt Castle (1454)

** Sigillu duc' norff edwardi nevyll.edmundi lentall'*
(The Seal of the Duke of Norfolk, Edward Neville, Edmund Lentall).

The armorial (heraldic) seals of John Charlton and Ithel ap Bleddyn are both characteristic of the early to mid-14th Century, the device being within a cusped Gothic panel. The lion rampant of Charlton had been an armorial device in Powys since the 11th century. The shield of Ap Bleddyn depicts two lions rampant, the crest (on a helmet) is a coroneted and draped maiden's head. The seal of Thomas Kemeys (unlike the later Kemeys arms) depicts a chevron, between two broad arrowheads and a cinquefoil. The shield of Holt Castle bears the arms, chequy, of the Howards, Dukes of Norfolk.

Female

21. Hawys, lady of Cyfeiliog (c.1300)

**S'HAWISIE DNE DE KEVEOLOC*
(The Seal of Hawys, lady of Cyfeiliog)

This seal, showing the lady Hawys arrayed in girdled dress and long cloak, and wearing a wimple and flat head-dress, is a good example of the usefulness of seals in illustrating contemporary costume.

Hawys (d.1300) was the wife either of Gruffydd ap Gwenwynwyn, or of John de Charlton (d. **c.**1350), who ruled Southern Powys and Cyfeiliog. The shield in her right hand displays a lion rampant, the arms of her husband; the two lions passant of the other shield, the arms of the Strange family, probably indicate her descent.

Religious

22. Agnus Dei (c.1300)

PRDIVE'SU
(. . . . . Jesu)

23. John the Baptist (c.1300)

**IOH'E.VOTV.PRECO.XPI SUSCIPE.TOTVM*
(John, herald of Christ, accept all our vow).

24. William ap David (? of Stanton, Gwent. 1451)
IESVS NAZARENVS ?
(Jesus of Nazareth)

25. Blessed Virgin Mary (1350)

S'COMMVNE·ABBATIS ET· . . NVENTVS DE ABERCONWV
(The Common Seal of the Abbot and Community of Aberconwy).

A very popular motif in the Middle Ages was the *Agnus Dei*, the Lamb of God, symbolic of Jesus Christ. In *Plate 22*, the seal, found at the site of Carmarthen Priory, shows the *Agnus Dei* borne by St. John the Baptist who baptised Jesus in the river Jordan. In *Plate 24*, the Crucified Christ is depicted between two kneeling suppliants. Another figure popular in the design of seals was that of the Blessed Virgin Mary bearing the Child Jesus: in *Plate 25*, an abbot of Aberconwy kneels before her.

Rural Life and Pursuits

The motifs employed on medieval seals frequently reflected the importance of hunting, both as a pastime and a means of obtaining food such as venison. On the seal of Geoffrey of Stormy a huntsman is blowing his horn; the prized deer is trying to escape at speed in the seal of Henry of Sutton; the weaponry of the age – the bow and arrow – is shown on that of Roger Grammus.

Hunting also served to put down destructive and ferocious animals. The extermination of the wolf was encouraged by Edward I in 1281. Walter Luvel derived his surname from the Latin *lupellus* (wolf) and displays the animal on his seal.

26. Geoffrey of Stormy (c.1170)

+ *SIGILLVM.GALFRID...STVRMI*
(The Seal of Geoffrey Sturmi)

27. Henry of Sutton (c.1290)

+ *S·HENRICI·DE·SVTTONE*
(The Seal of Henry de Sutton)

28. Roger Grammus of Kenfig (c.1200)

+ *SIGILL'.ROGERI.GRAMVS*
(The Seal of Roger Grammus)

29. Walter Luvel of Llangewydd (1202)

+ *SIGILLVM:WALTERI:LVWEL*
(The Seal of Walter Luvel)

All these four seals are of Welsh gentry living in the neighbourhood of Margam and Kenfig. These, and those shown opposite, are largely of the circular type utilised widely for personal seals by the laity.

Miscellaneous Devices

30. Kynwric ap Heylyn (of Cilcain)
(1304)

+ *S':KINWRIC.F.HEILIN*
(The Seal of Kynwric, son of Heylyn)

31. Hywel Gogh of Tremeirchion
(1352)

* *S'HOWEL F'HOWEL*
(The Seal of Hywel, son of Hywel).

These two seals are typical of many circular, personal seals of the early 14th century from N.E. Wales. They depict ears of wheat, conjoined at the stalk, and reflect the agrarian society of the period.

32. Member of the Pincerna family
(of Morgan) (1218)

+ *SIGILLVM . . . . . . I. PINCERNA*
(The Seal of . . . . . . Butler).

An example of a seal displaying the occupation which lent the family its name. In this case the seal depicts a butler (in Latin, *'pincerna'*) with a drinking cup in his hand. The Butlers (or Butilers) were lords of Marcross in the thirteenth century.

33. Madog ap Knaytho (of Morgan)
c.1225.

+ *SIGILL':MADOCI:FILII:KANAITH'*
(The Seal of Madog, son of Knaytho).

The 'fleur-de-lis' or 'flower of Louis', another common medieval device on seals, was associated with the crusading spirit. The flower is an iris, said to have had been adopted by Louis VII of France as his emblem when setting out on his Crusade (1146).

Significance of The Seal: Use of Several Seals

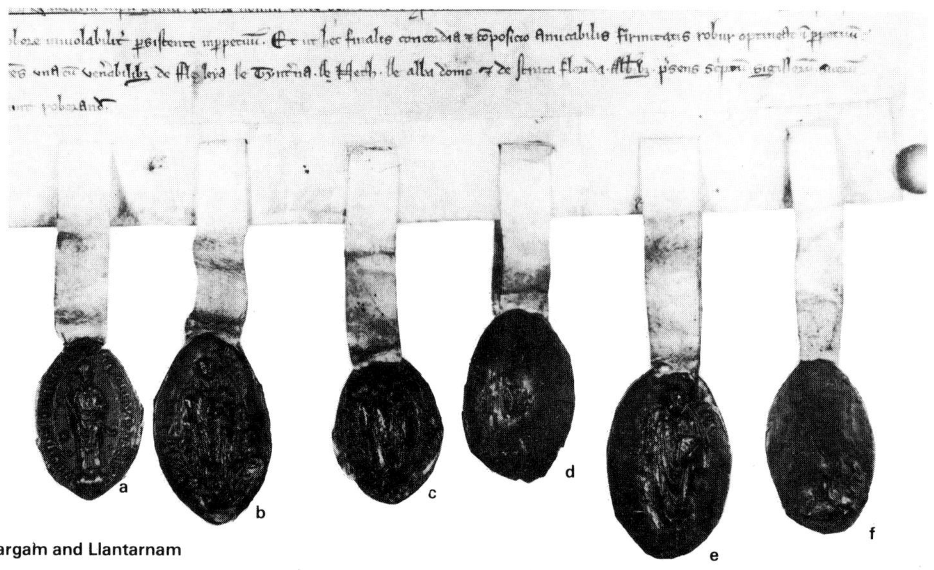

34. Agreement between Margam and Llantarnam Abbeys (1256)

(Seals of abbots of (**a**) Margam, (**b**) Tintern, (**c**) Neath, (**d**) Whitland, (**e**)/(**f**) Strata Florida and Flaxley).

Important documents were frequently attested by the affixing of the seals of several arbitrators or witnesses, so giving greater force to the deed concerned. Sometimes, the seals were placed from left to right in order of the precedence of their owners. The six seals attached to this manuscript, the settlement of a territorial dispute between the two Cistercian abbeys of Margam and Llantarnam, would make the agreement difficult to dispute, contradict or infringe in years to come. The closing lines reflect this purpose: *"And, so that this final agreement and friendly arrangement may obtain strength of firmness for ever, the abbots of the said houses, together with the venerable abbots of Flaxley, Tintern, Neath, Whitland and of Strata Florida, have caused the present deed to be confirmed with the impressions of their seals."*

Two copies of the agreement were sealed, the other would have borne the seal of the abbot of Llantarnam (*alias* Caerleon). The upper edge of the document displayed here has an indented edge corresponding to that on the other copy (retained by Margam). The authenticity of both parts could be demonstrated in later years by fitting them together.

Significance of The Seal: Care and Custody

The importance of the seal meant that steps were often taken to protect it against casual damage. The monks of Ewenny Priory safeguarded the seal of the Anglo-Norman knight who had given them land, by placing it in this green silk bag. Important seals of dignity, including the Great Seals of England, were similarly kept in silk bags.

A corporate seal, such as that of a monastic community, might be kept in such a way that no one individual had access to it: this guarded against improper use. In Tudor times, the common seal of the Radnorshire abbey of Cwmhir was "wont to be kept in a chest with two locks, the key of the one lock remaining with the abbot, and the other with one of the monks especially appointed for that purpose." In 1558 Archdeacon John Smith of Llandaff confessed that "he once broke the coffer and took out thereof the chapter seal contrary to the Bishop's will". In 1568 the common seal of the newly-established Friars School at Bangor was ordered to be kept in a chest with two locks in the Cathedral Chapter House, the key to the one lock remaining with the Bishop, the other with the Dean and Chapter.

Official seals of the Crown were often handed over with great ceremony. When, in 1343, the Commissioners of the Black Prince delivered a new seal of office to the Chamberlain of the Exchequer at Caernarfon, it was done in the presence of a great company headed by the bishop of Bangor. The significance of the seal was reflected in the proclamation made that the old seal was of no avail, and it was deposited in the king's chancery. Again, this was to guard against fraudulent use of the former seal; sometimes expired seals were broken up, melted down or, more usually, defaced. The seals of the later Courts of Great Sessions in Wales (see page 32) had official Custodians appointed.

35. Gilbert de Turberville (Early 13th Century)

Significance of The Seal: The Welsh Princes

36. Llywelyn ab Iorwerth (1208)

. . . *SIGIL* . . . . . . *IPI* . . . . . .
(The Seal of . . . . . . Prince . . . . . .)

The thirteenth century in Wales has been called the 'age of the two Llywelyns', for its political history was dominated by Llywelyn ab Iorwerth (Llywelyn the Great), Prince of Gwynedd (1194-1240), and his grandson, Prince Llywelyn ab Gruffydd (Llywelyn the Last, 1246-82). The first Llywelyn rose to ascendancy in Gwynedd whilst a young man in his twenties, and then turned his attention further afield. Before his thirtieth birthday (1203) his authority stretched from the Dyfi to the Dee. He married Joan, the daughter of King John (1205), but spent much of his time fighting her father's army. This conflict continued into the reign of Henry III, reaching its climax in Llywelyn's invasion of South Wales (1231), which has been called a "hurricane of war", and in his partnership with the rebel baron, Richard Marshal (1233). A prolonged truce followed until Llywelyn's death and burial in the Cistercian abbey at Aberconwy (1240).

Under Llywelyn's leadership, fighting was mainly limited to the Border areas and to South Wales; in most of North Wales, and especially in Gwynedd and Southern Powys, conditions of peace and relative prosperity prevailed. It was a time of considerable literary activity – the poets flourished, and the compilation of prose tales known as the *Mabinogion* may date from this period. It was an age which saw the emergence of the Venedotion Code, an edition of the laws of Hywel the Good which incorporated Gwynedd usages. It was a season which saw the appointment of Welsh bishops in the Church, as Cadwgan at Bangor in 1215 (**cf. Plate 57**), and the granting of important confirmatory Charters to the Cistercian monasteries of Aberconwy, possibly as early as 1199, and to Cymer in 1209.

By no means the least of Llywelyn's achievements was the fact that he did much "to win over the people of Wales to the view that they were sharers in a single political and cultural inheritance." He achieved his position, however, only by ousting his uncles Dafydd and Rhodri, and, later, by finally capturing Southern Powys from prince Gwenwynwyn, who took his own name from its constituent commote of Cyfeiliog. On the English front, Llywelyn's success partly lay in taking advantage of discord between both John and, after him, Henry III and their barons.

It is from the age of Llywelyn ab Iorwerth and Gwenwynwyn that the earliest known Welsh seals mostly date. Their charters to Strata Marcella Abbey, near Welshpool, underline the importance attached to the seal in medieval days. Gwenwynwyn confirmed one of his gifts, so that it could not later be challenged, 'with the protection of my seal.' One of the objects of the design of a seal was that it should be distinguishable from these of other people, so Llywelyn ratified his grant 'with the peculiar (*i.e.* especial) impression of my seal.'

Great persons in this period often used green wax when impressing and attaching their seals to important documents. Both the 'great' seals depicted here (**Plates 36 and 37**) are 'equestrian' seals, portraying their owners armed and on horseback, a reminder of their ability to do battle. Such persons often also had a smaller 'privy' or 'secret' seal. This was usually applied to the reverse of the 'great' seal, giving it even greater authenticity and force. Llywelyn's was so applied (**Plate 38**) on the occasion of his daughter, Helen, marrying a nephew of the Earl of Chester, John the Scot (1222). Llywelyn sometimes used it separately, explaining, on one occasion, that he was 'sealing the letters with his secret seal, because he has not his great seal with him.'

There are no known impressions extant of the seal of Llywelyn the Last (1246-82), but – almost as if to ensure that it could not be used improperly – the privy seal of this Llywelyn, together with those of his wife, Eleanor, and his brother, prince David, were melted down in 1284 on the orders of Edward I, whose Conquest of Wales (*see later*) was more or less complete. All three had lately died, all three were persons of significance, and their privy seals, which were of silver, were turned into a chalice.

37. Gwenwynwyn of Powys (1205)

SIGILL · GWENWNWIN · DE · KEVEILIAVC
(The Seal of Gwenwynwyn of Cyfeiliog)

38. Privy Seal of Llywelyn ab Iorwerth (1222)

+ *SIGILLVM SECRETVM LEVLINI·*
(The Secret Seal of Llywelyn)
(a boar under a tree)

Anglo-Norman Settlement

The Norman Conquest of England was followed by a series of incursions into Wales from castles built in the Marches at strategic points. Norman lords made their mark, amongst them Robert Fitzhamon in Glamorgan and Bernard de Newmarch in Brecknock. Welsh princes were held in captivity – as Gruffydd ap Cynan of Gwynedd (1087), or killed – as Iestyn Morgannwg and Rhys ap Tewdwr of Deheubarth (both in 1093). Knights who served under the Norman barons were rewarded with grants of confiscated land, boroughs were established near to the new castles, and foreign monks were settled in urban priories. In the twelfth century, the Welsh made a considerable comeback, especially after the death of Henry I (1135). Under leaders such as Owain Gwynedd (d.1170) and the Lord Rhys in Ceredigion (d.1197), much of North and West Wales returned to Welsh rule, although the South and South-East remained primarily a Norman sphere. This division, upheld by princes such as the two Llywelyns, was to more or less hold good until the Edwardian Conquest a century later. The twelfth-century resurgence of Welsh power provided a suitable climate for the establishment of Cistercian foundations in North and West Wales, allied to the national cause.

After the death of Henry I, the accession of King Stephen, a grandson of William I, was contested in open conflict by Stephen's cousin, Empress Matilda of the Holy Roman (German) Empire, who was Henry's daughter and preferred heir. For a few years (**c.**1141-47) she held suzerainty over part of Western England and much of the Marches. Her seal shown here is attached to the deed by which she granted her close ally, Earl Milo of Hereford, the Castle and Lordship of Abergavenny. The de Clares, too, held substantial lands in Wales from 1110 onwards. Earl Gilbert, 5th Earl of Gloucester and Hertford (1216-30), was also Lord of Usk, Wentloog and Glamorgan. His shield displays the family arms: three chevrons. *(For the obverse of this seal see page 10).*

39. The Empress Matilda, 'lady of England'. (1141-2)

+ S'MATHILDE .... ROM ....
(The Seal of Matilda, ... Queen of the Romans).

40. Gilbert de Clare
(5th Earl of Gloucester, **c.**1220).

SIGILL.GILEBERTI.DE.CLARA: COMITIS:GLOVERNIE
(The Seal of Gilbert de Clare, Earl of Gloucester).

The Edwardian Conquest

After the death of prince David (1246), his nephew Llywelyn ap Gruffydd not only continued to resist the sallies of Henry III, but also used the disturbed political circumstances to establish his own princely authority well beyond the confines of North Wales. The result was that the Peace of Montgomery (1267) left Llywelyn with suzerainty and influence over the greater part of Wales, with the title 'Prince of Wales'. In the early years of Edward I's reign, however, Llywelyn refused to pay either homage or financial dues to the new sovereign, and this eventually led to an English siege of the prince's natural fortress of Snowdonia. Llywelyn, cut off from supplies of food, was forced to submit. At the subsequent Treaty of Aberconwy (1277) he lost much of his conquered territory and feudal authority.

The next war arose partly out of Welsh resentment, not of the monarch himself, but of the oppressive practices of his officials in Wales, and was sparked off by Llywelyn's brother, David, now disaffected with the English. Prince David made a surprise night attack on Hawarden Castle in March 1282, and Llywelyn was quick to join the fray, which was conducted on a wide front. Edward's army again approached both by sea and land, but suffered a humiliating defeat at the Menai Straits. Late in the year, Llywelyn, who had travelled to Breconshire to raise the Welshry there, was killed whilst separated from his troops (Dec. 11th, 1282); his head was sent for public display in London, his body buried at Abbey Cwmhir. Prince David continued the struggle, but was hunted down, captured in Snowdonia (June, 1283) and a little later executed at Shrewsbury.

The leaders dead, resistance crumbled: Edward had conquered Wales. He set up a chain of castles to help preserve peace, he appointed new officials, notably the Justice of North Wales, to assist in exercising royal authority and, in 1284, he made a royal progress through Wales. National feeling was by no means dead: King Edward had to quell lesser revolts, the chief being those of Rhys ap Maredudd in Carmarthenshire (1287), and of Madog, Prince Llywelyn's son, who temporarily took Caernarfon (1294). However, by 1301 Edward I was able, with some political justification, to create his eldest son Prince of Wales. The obverse of his seal is reproduced here.

41. Edward, Prince of Wales (c.1305)

EDWARDUS ILLVSTRIS REGIS ANGLIE FILIVS
(Edward, son of the renowned King of England)

Welsh Nobility and Gentry

The Welsh resurgence in the later twelfth century, and the military strength of the two Llywelyns in the thirteenth, re-established Welsh rule over large areas of the country. Welsh nobles and gentry emerged as men of influence, either because (as in Central Wales) they opposed the new order, or because (as in South Wales) they lived uneasily side by side with it. Such men included Maredudd ab Hywel, associated with resistance in Powys to Henry II, and a benefactor of Strata Marcella Abbey; and Lleision ap Morgan, who (**c.**1204) commanded two hundred Welshmen in Afan, and was a patron of Margam Abbey.

Perhaps copying the Normans, the Welsh nobility, like their Princes, came to have seals of some size and quality; often these were impressed in the costly green wax much used in the seals of the early 13th century (see the Seals of Prince Llywelyn ab Iorwerth and Bishop Cadwgan of Bangor: **Plates 36 and 57**). Like the Normans they often favoured an equestrian seal. Lleision ap Morgan had a second seal showing him kneeling before the Abbot of Margam, perhaps symbolising that certain differences he had with the monastery had been resolved. It is important for showing details of the dress of a Welsh gentleman of the period, as is the fine seal of the flower or flame carrying Gilbert Burdin.

¾ actual size

42. Maredudd ab Hywel (1176)
(Lord of Edeyrnion).

+ *SIGILLU .... L*
(The Seal of ....

43. Lleision ap Morgan
(**c.**1220) (Lord of Afan).

+
SIGILLVM:LEISAVN:FILII:MORGAN
(The Seal of Lleision, the son of Morgan).

44. Gilbert Burdin (of Morgan).
(**ca.**1200)

SIGILLVM.GILLEBERTI:BVRDINI
(The Seal of Gilbert Burdin).

45. Lleision ap Morgan (ç.1220).

..... GILLVM LEISAN:FI ......
(The Seal of Lleision, the son of ......).

The Glyn Dŵr Revolt

46. **Owain Glyn Dŵr** (1404)
(obverse of the Great Seal)

· *owynus . . . . princeps·wallie*
(Owain . . . . prince of Wales)

Among the upper ranks of the Welsh gentry in the year 1400 was an educated lawyer, aged about 45, of military experience and ability. He was Owain Glyn Dŵr, of princely descent, and master of Glyn Dyfrdwy and Cynllaith, two lordships in North Wales. Proclaimed Prince of Wales on September 16th by a group of relatives and friends, he led a devastating uprising against the English establishment. Cardiff was burnt in 1403; in 1404, the rebels took Harlech and Aberystwyth Castles, and Owain held a Parliament at Machynlleth. In 1405 2,500 French troops landed at Milford Haven, augmenting Owain's 10,000 men, and making possible a temporary foray into England. This was the peak of the Revolt: from 1406 there were more reverses than successes.

The treaty his envoys negotiated with King Charles VI of France in 1404 preserves in Paris to-day Owain's great seal, his privy seal being attached to their commission (**Plate 1**). On the obverse of the great seal (**46**) Owain is shown bearded, holding a sceptre but uncrowned. On the reverse, the Welsh dragon appears on his helmet and on his horse's head. His privy seal summed up his ancestry and his aspirations, displaying, as it did, four lions rampant – the ancient royal arms of Gwynedd.

47. **Richard Gethin** (1438)

Richard Gethyn

During the protracted Hundred Years War, many Welshmen served in the English army or as Crown officials; amongst them was Sir Richard Gethin, Bailiff of Eureux, Normandy. His arms were a chevron between three falcons rising.

Medieval Boroughs and Ports

One lasting consequence of Edward I's Conquest of Wales lay in his building a series of castles at strategic points. In many cases a borough was established near the castle, regularly with a substantial number of English immigrants, whose presence bolstered English authority. A number of the new boroughs lay near the sea; their seals, therefore, often bear a ship on the obverse side, a castle on the reverse.

48. Conwy (1426)

**S'PROVESTRIE:DE:CONEWEY*
(The Seal of the Provost of Conwy)

In the spring of 1283, Édward I stayed at the Cistercian abbey of Aberconwy. The following year he moved the monks seven miles upstream to Maenan, to make way for the building of a castle and borough at this important position at the mouth of the Conwy. The seal depicts both castle and tidal water. It was at Conwy Castle that Prince Edward received the homage of the Welsh people in 1301.

49. Denbigh (1285)

+ S'CŌMVNE:BVRGENSIV̄:DE:DINBEY
(The Common Seal of the Burgesses of Denbigh)

Denbigh Castle, probably the site of a Welsh fortification of great antiquity, was the location for a parliament held by Prince David in 1282. In the same year, after the Conquest, the Castle was rebuilt by Henry de Lacy on the orders of Edward I, and the borough of Denbigh became an important centre of English settlement. Its seal is unusual in that it is unfinished, its upper portion remaining blank.

50. Harlech (1549)

**SIGILLV:COMMVNE:DE:HARDLECH*
(The Common Seal of Harlech)

The commanding position of Harlech Castle, on its rock overlooking Cardigan bay, is well known.

Decayed Boroughs

Not all boroughs were the result of the Edwardian Conquest: some, like Kenfig, reflected earlier Anglo-Norman settlement. Not all boroughs continued to flourish: Kenfig again, founded as a port and castle town about 1180, eventually succumbed to the encroachment of blown sand. Newborough, in Anglesey, although granted a charter (1303) and the right to appoint a mayor provided he was an Englishman (1347), remained without a castle. Edward Lhuyd was able to record of Trellech, Gwent, in about 1700, that it was 'formerly a market town, and had a mayor for its chief officer, but now is reduced to a poore inconsiderable village.'

The common seal of Kenfig displays a quatrefoil between four pellets. The seal of Newborough shows three fishes; a similar device may have been employed by the borough of Nevin. This seal has also been attributed to Newport (Gwent) and Newport (Salop). Another Newborough seal (1426) depicted a single-masted ship. The seal of Trellech bore three chevrons, the arms of the de Clares, Earls of Gloucester and Lords of Usk. The seal of the Porter of Cardiff is a good example of a device, on this occasion a key, reflecting the occupation of its owner.

51. Kenfig (c.1250)

+ *S':CŌMVNE:DE:KENEḞ'*
(The Common Seal of Kenfig)

52. Newborough (14th Century)

+ . . . . *NOVA* . . . . *BVRGA* . . . .
(. . . . New . . . . Borough . . . .)

53. Trellech (13th Century)

+ *S':COMMVNITATIS:BVRGI·DE TRILL'.*
(The Seal of the Commonalty of the Borough of Trellech).

54. Porter of the Town Gate of Cardiff
(Early 13th Century)

+ *SIGILLVM·ADE·PORTARI*
(The Seal of Adam the Porter)

Ports

55. Tenby (14/15th Centuries).

+ *Sigillum:comune:burgensium:ville:tenebie*
(The Common Seal of the burgesses of Tenby)

The port of Tenby, granted a charter in 1290, was significant in the Middle Ages for the importation of wine, and the exportation of cloth and hides. It maintained commercial links with Brittany, and eventually became a centre of piracy. It was the port at which Jasper Tudor embarked for France after the Lancastrian defeat of 1471.

The role of Tenby as a fortified port is reflected in its seal. The obverse bears a ship of the period in full sail. The reverse exhibits a gate with a portcullis, flanked by two towers and bearing arms derived from the De Valences, previous Earls of Pembroke.

56. Monmouth (1616)

+ *COMMVNE.SIGILL'.MONEMVTE*
(The Common Seal of Monmouth)

The single-masted vessel, resembling a Viking ship, depicted on this seal of the 13th Century, reflects Monmouth's importance for much of the Middle Ages as an inland port. Supplies for the Earl of Lancaster's castle, such as wine from Bristol, came to the town by boats plying on the river Wye. More than one fourteenth century dispute arose from fishing weirs impeding navigation on the river. A new seal, still bearing a ship as its device was in use from 1675.

The Medieval Church

Bishops and Cathedral Chapters

The coming of the Normans to Wales meant for the Celtic Church submission to the authority of Rome, acknowledgement of the primacy of Canterbury, transfer of church dedications from Welsh to European saints, an end to the 'clas' form of monasticism, and – another sore point – the intrusion of alien clerics as bishops in Welsh sees.

There were, however, notable Welsh bishops – not least Cadwgan of Bangor, a former abbot of Whitland, a spiritual preacher and writer of consequence.

The use of green wax in his seal (**57**) is reminiscent of the seals of Llywelyn and Gwenwynwyn (**36** and **37**). It is a typical early episcopal seal, simple in style. The later seal of Bishop Adam (**58**) is far more elaborate. It depicts St Andrew (secondary patron) and St David, with Christ in majesty (above), the bishop (below), flanked by shields displaying the arms of England (left) and of the Houghton family (right).

Cathedral Chapters, as corporate bodies, had their own proper seals: the first seal of Llandaff (**59**) attempts to exhibit the Cathedral as built by Bishop Urban (**c.**1130).

57. Cadwgan, Bishop of Bangor (1215-36)

. . . M:CADVCANI . . . . . EPISCOPI:BANGORENS . . .
(The Seal of Cadwgan, Bishop of Bangor).

58. Adam Houghton, Bishop of St David's (1361-89)

SIGILL':A . . . . . . MENEVNS':EP̄I:
(The Seal of Adam, Bishop of Menevia).

¾ actual size

59. Llandaff Cathedral Chapter (**c.**1200)

+ SIGILLVM. LANDAVENSIS. ECCLESIE
(The Seal of the Church of Llandaff)

Ecclesiastical Officials and Institutions

The medieval Church enjoyed uniformity of doctrine and, to a large extent, of worship; but within its essential unity lay a diversity of institutional life. Such religious institutions included collegiate churches, served by a number of prebendaries who resided often for only part of the year, and hospitals – homes for sick and poor people under the care of a master. Many early hospitals were leper-houses which, as leprosy waned, became alms-houses and hospices.

60. Urban, Archdeacon of Llandaff (c.1190-1200)

+ *SIGILLV̄.VRBANI.ARCHDIAC.LANDAVIE*
(The Seal of Urban, Archdeacon of Llandaff).

Archdeacon Urban, the principal official and right-hand man of two bishops of Llandaff, was a witness to several charters granting land to Margam Abbey. His seal displays a dove, perhaps as a symbol of peace or the Holy Spirit.

61. St David's Hospital, Swansea (1548).

SIGILLVM COE·DOM:BEATI DAVID DE:SWEYNESE
(The Common Seal of the House of Blessed David of Swansea)

St. David's Hospital, Swansea, was built in 1330 for the welfare of poor infirm clerics and layfolk. Six chaplains, under a Master, were to provide daily services in the Chapel. A Warden, two priests and at least four poor men, still lived there in 1548.

62. Abergwili Collegiate Church

**S'precentoris et capitili ecclesie collegiate-de-abergwily*
(The Seal of the Precentor and Chapter of the Collegiate Church of Abergwili)

The dedication of this College to St Maurice shows Norman influence. Founded at Llangadog in 1283, it was moved to Abergwili about 1292. It had 22 prebendaries. This seal-die, discovered in Leicestershire (**see p.5**), dates from after 1334, when the post of precentor was established.

Monastic Life

Latin monasticism entered Wales in the wake of the Norman Conquest (**p.20**). Benedictine priories were often founded, as at Brecon, in the protective shadow of the new castles. Goldcliff, lying by the Severn Estuary, was an exception. A cell of Bec in Normandy, all its monks came from France, and unlike the 'black monks' of Brecon, they wore white habits. Several other Orders were represented in Wales – amongst them the Institution of Bonshommes in Ruthin, and the Augustinian Canons at Llanthony.

The seal of Brecon Priory shows an eagle (for St John the Evangelist, its patron) standing on a demi-wheel (from the prophecy of Ezekiel). The seal of Goldcliff shows its patron (St Mary Magdalene) carrying a vase of oil, meeting the risen Lord in the Garden on Easter Day. The seal of Llanthony depicts the Baptism of Christ in the Jordan, on his right John the Baptist, on his left an angel; above the Holy Spirit descends as a dove. The seal of Ruthin Priory displays a key-bearing St Peter with (below) the arms of the founders, the Grey family, barry of six, in chief three roundles.

63. Brecon Priory, (1514)
(Benedictine)

Sigillum·conventuale·domus:sci·
iohis·ewangeliste·de brechoīe
(The Conventual Seal of the House of St. John the Evangelist of Brecon)

64. Goldcliff Priory (1340)
(Benedictine)

(The legend of the Goldcliff Priory seal is almost entirely illegible)

65. St Peter's Priory, Ruthin
(1465) (Bonshommes)

SIG'COMMVNE·DOMVS SCI·PETRI
DE·RVTHYN
(The Common Seal of the House of St Peter of Ruthin).

66. Llanthony Priory (Gwent)
(1316) (Augustinian)

+ *SIGILLVM . . . . . . E:SCA· . . . . . .*
E·LANTHONIA
(The Common Seal of St . . . .,
Llanthony).

The Cistercian Order in Wales: Evolution of the Seal

The religious order which found most sympathy in Wales was the Cistercian Order, the 'White Monks'. In the thirteenth century, the abbots of at least four Cistercian houses acted as intermediaries between English monarchs and Welsh princes.

The design of the early seals of the Order was governed by various rulings of its annual general chapter. In the thirteenth century, each house used an abbot's seal which depicted either a cowled wrist and hand grasping a pastoral staff (**67**), or else the abbot full-length (**68**). In the fourteenth century, by royal statute and papal decree, every house had a common seal bearing an image of the Blessed Virgin Mary. That of Basingwerk (**69**) bears additionally the initials *H. W.* for Henry Wirral, abbot 1430-54, and still used here by his successor. The Seal of Margam (**70**) is ornamented with the arms (*left*) of Robert, Earl of Gloucester, its founder (three clarions), and (*right*) of the de Clares, later Lords of Glamorgan (three chevrons – **see p.30**). For another Cistercian seal design, an abbot kneeling before the Blessed Virgin, (**see No. 25**).

A further development in seal design came after the short-lived restoration of Strata Florida in 1537, when a new seal was prepared engraved with the royal arms; the same may have also been the case at Neath and Whitland.

67. Tintern (1245)

+ SIGILLVM·ABBATIS DE TINTERNA
(The Seal of the Abbot of Tintern)

68. Neath (1266)

+ SIGILLV . . . ABBA . . . TH:
(The Seal of the Abbot of Neath)

69. Basingwerk (1465)

+ . . . m·conventus·de·basyngwerke·
(The Convent Seal of Basingwerk)

70. Margam (1525)

+ SIGILLVM:ABBATIS:ET:CONV-ENTVS:DE:MARGAN
(The Seal of the Abbot and Convent of Margam)

Counter-Seals

As with the use of privy seals by persons such as prince Llywelyn (**p.19**), the common seals of several monasteries were given greater authority and security in their use, by the impressing of the abbot's own seal as a counter-seal on the reverse.

A late 16th century collection of copies of leases granted by the former abbey of Cwmhir, noted of abbot Richard Vaughan's seal (1516-30) that it 'ought to have upon the backside three small seals, every of them *v* square' an obscure statement, perhaps meaning '*four* square' as is the arrangement of the impressions illustrated here. A seal of the abbot of Strata Florida from the same period (**71**) bears on the reverse three such seals, each displaying – in this case, a two-headed eagle and the legend *'R. Dorston'.* They are the counter-seals of abbot Richard Dorston (1513), formerly abbot of Grace Dieu (1486-88) and of Dore (1495-1500).

An early counter-seal of Whitland (**72**) bears the abbatial device of a hand grasping a pastoral staff.

Abbot John Gruffydd of Grace Dieu (1534-36) had a counter-seal displaying his initials (**73**); so did his namesake at Margam (1517-28, No. **11**); they may, indeed, have been one and the same person, but the seals are different.

71. Strata Florida (1513)
(enlarged)

R. dorston
(R ichard Dorston)

72. Whitland (1303)

+ *CONTRA SIGILL' ALBE . . . VS*
(The Counterseal of the White House)

73. Grace Dieu (1535)

I. G.
(John Gruffydd)

Act of Union (1536)

The Act of Union of 1536, uniting England and Wales, supplemented by a further act in 1542, established county boundaries in the Principality which endured until 1974. To counter the prevalent state of lawlessness in parts of Wales, the country (Monmouthshire excepted) was dividend into four judicial circuits of three counties each, for the purpose of the Great Sessions. George Owen told how "thear is in every sheere a great sessions or assisses houlden every yeare twyce, and a justice of assise for every three sheeres."

74. Judicial Seal for Denbigh, Montgomery and Flint. (1545) (obverse)

HENRIC'·VIII·DEI·GR̄A·ANGLIE·FR̄AC·ƶ· HIBN̄E·
REX:FIDEI:DEFĒS:ET·IN·T'RA
ECCL·AGL·Z·HIB̄NICE·SVPREM̄·CAPVT
(Henry VIII, by the Grace of God, King of England, France, and Ireland: Defender of the Faith, and, in the lands of England and Ireland, Supreme Head of the Church.)

Each circuit had its own Judicial Seal which (on the obverse) displayed the monarch on horseback, and (on the reverse) a shield of the royal arms, with the Prince of Wales feathers at the base. The supporters to the shields differed: in the case of Denbigh, Montgomery and Flint, they were (left) a stag gorged with a coronet, (right) a lion rampant guardant crowned. The 'Method of Proceeding in the Court of Great Sessions for Glamorgan, Brecon and Radnor' (1817; NLW MS 3854B) provided that there should be an Original Seal for issuing writs and a Judicial Seal for witnessing judicial process.

(reverse)

+ S + IVDICIALE + DNI + REGIS + PRO COMITATIBVS + DENBIGHE + MONTGOMERI + ET + FLINT
(The Judicial Seal of the Lord King for the Counties of Denbigh, Montgomery, and Flint)

Seal Engravers

The costly official seals of royal government for Wales were engraved in London. Nicholas de Twyford, a London goldsmith was in 1377, during the minority of Thomas le Despenser, paid £5. 10. 0. for engraving and making a seal ordered by King Edward III for the lordships of Glamorgan and Morgannwg. Shortly after the accession of Henry V in 1413 John Bernes, another London goldsmith, received £10 for engraving two pairs of double seals for the principalities of North and South Wales.

In 1687 Thomas East, engraver to James II, presented an account for £340 for the engraving of several seals necessitated by the accession of that monarch. They included two Chancery and two Judicial seals for Welsh counties. The bill for the Judicial Seal for Denbigh, Montgomery and Flint is reproduced here. To East is also attributed the first Great Seal of James II, which was lost in the Thames during the King's flight in December 1688.

For a large double Judiciall Seale of Silver for the Counties of Denbigh, Montgomery and fflint, Ingraven with his Mat^ts Effigies on horsback in Armor over a Landscap, and a plumb of feathers placed behind him with the Motto ICH: DIEN: having his Ma^ts Titles in the Circumference.

On the other side his Ma^ts Royall Coat of Armes in a shield with a Compartment an Imperiall Crowne over, and a plumb of ffeathers with ICH: DIEN: under, supported by a Lyon Crowned on the one side, and an Antilop Gorged with a Crowne and Chayned on the other side, in the Circumference. — SIGILVM: IVDICIALE: PRO: COMITIBVS: DENBII: MONTGOMERI: ET: FLINT: 1686. Weighing in Silver oz dw 27:06 at 5:6 p Ounce - - - - - -

	£ s d
	60 : 00 : 00
	07 : 10 : 00
ffor a large Shagreene Case to keep it in - -	02 : 00 : 00
	69 : 10 : 00

75. Account of Thomas East (1687)

The Shires

The effects of the Acts of Union were considerable in Wales, not least in that the Celtic system of inheritance, *gavelkind*, whereby a dead man's property was shared amongst all his sons, was replaced by *primogeniture* in which the eldest son inherited his father's lands. The Acts also militated against the Welsh language, for they insisted upon English being used in courts of law in Wales.

The remaining medieval Marcher Lordships were abolished, and henceforth 'the shire was the chief unit of local government, not only in legal but in administrative matters'. The chief official of the shire was the sheriff, 'whose duties embraced every aspect of local government, from the collecting of royal dues to the policing of the

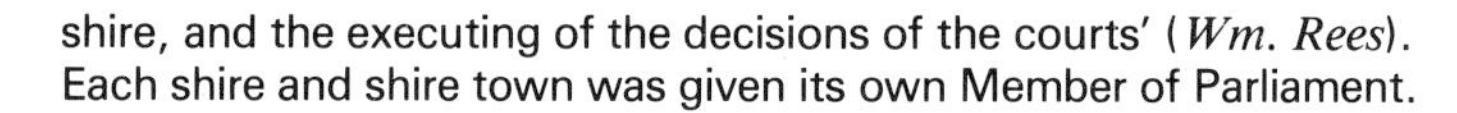

shire, and the executing of the decisions of the courts' (*Wm. Rees*). Each shire and shire town was given its own Member of Parliament.

Each shire was divided into 'Hundreds' under the jurisdiction of Justices of the Peace (eight in each county) who held the Hundred Court or 'Petty Sessions', to deal with minor infringements of the law. Four times a year they met together to try more serious offences at the 'Quarter Sessions.'

The counties had no common seals until the much later Local Government Act of 1888 (**see p.41**). The sheriffs, therefore, used their own personal seals. Thomas Bowen, Sheriff of Breconshire in 1687, appears to have used someone else's seal (**76**). John Sparrow Sheriff of Anglesey in 1708, punned on his surname in the arms displayed on his seal: a chevron between three sparrows (**77**).

76. Sheriff of Brecon (1687)
H.W.

(enlarged)

77. Sheriff of Anglesey (1708)

Industrial Revolution

Coal, Iron and Steel

The reign of Elizabeth I (1558-1603) saw fresh impetus given to industry and trade in Wales. Brass works were set up at Tintern, copper was smelted at Neath and iron at Merthyr, whilst Pembrokeshire had flourishing coal exports. The pace of industry accelerated with the opening of the Dowlais and Cyfarthfa iron works in 1758 and 1765, which utilized local ore and charcoal. The proximity of coal soon made this the more important fuel, and, aided by the construction of canals and later of railways, the South Wales Coalfield made its name both for mining and industry. By 1860, ten million tons of coal were mined each year, and by 1872 over a million tons of iron ore were produced. This was, of course, long before the days of nationalisation, and the individual companies concerned had their own corporate seals, some of them illustrative of their industry.

The Glamorgan Coal Company was founded in 1860, the prime mover in the enterprise being a Scotsman, Archibald Hood. Collieries were opened in the Rhondda (1861-72), which soon had a combined output of over 4,000 tons per day. The Company provided its workmen with housing and encouraged social and educational activity. Its seal displayed a surface coal-wagon, with brake-lever, bearing three Scotch thistles on its side. Shortly after Hood's death in 1902, D.A. Thomas, later Lord Rhondda, acquired (1907) an almost exclusive interest in the Company.

The Rhymney Iron Company was formed in 1836 by the amalgamation of the Union (1802) and Bute (1825) Works, which lay on opposite sides of the river Rhymney close to the Breconshire-Glamorgan boundary. The seal engraved in 1871 incorporates this date and gives an impression of a blacksmith or iron worker, suitably stripped for the purpose, hammering out iron in a forge.

The Blaenavon Iron Works was established in 1789, and within a decade its three blast furnaces were employing 350 men. After a long and by no means trouble-free history, the Blaenavon Iron and Steel Company emerged in 1870. Its seal depicts (in the foreground) a blast furnace, two pit-head frames with winding gear, and (in the background) an engine-house.

¾ actual size

78. Glamorgan Coal Co. (1930)

79. Rhymney Iron Co. (1937)

80. Blaenavon Iron and Steel Co. (1876)

Communications

The development of mining and industry brought with it a need for adequate communications. The second half of the 18th Century saw the development of roads in Wales by the many turnpike trusts. Even so, road conditions were often poor, and the tolls charged were a considerable burden. Towards the close of the century came the 'Canal Age' in Wales. Canals were important for moving heavy, bulky loads at a time when roads were inadequate and railways still undeveloped.

Welsh canals were limited in size and scope by the gradients, which demanded many locks, and often supplementary tram-roads to act as links with mining and industrial areas the canals could not reach. Several hundred miles of tram-roads were built in South Wales between 1800 to 1830. Built at first on stone blocks, not wooden sleepers, they were of limited usefulness, as their motive power was the horse. They were, however, easier and cheaper to construct than the canals, which they sometimes came to supersede. Further, they gave birth to the vast railway network developed in Wales in the later nineteenth century, the foundations of which were laid in the 'Railway Age' of 1840-60. The railways in their turn stimulated the construction of major docks, as at Cardiff and Newport.

The individual turnpike roads were managed by trustees. These groups of people did not have a common seal, each person affixing his own seal to trust deeds. The companies who managed the later means of communication did require to have common seals, and these are often of considerable interest. Many can be seen at the National Railway Museums in Swindon and York.

81. Monmouthshire Canal Co. (1792)

82. Sirhowy Tram Road Co. (1802)

83. Dulas Valley Mineral Railway Co. (1862)

The Monmouthshire Canal, the work of Thomas Dadford, had two branches, leading from Crumlin (1794) and Pontnewynydd (1796). Its main function was the conveyance of coal to Newport, whose coal exports rose from 18,000 tons in 1799 to 150,000 by 1810. The Company seal (**81**) shows Newport Castle between the river Usk (foreground) and the Canal (background), a horse-drawn barge, the early dock basin in Friars Fields (1804), and the hilly topography complete the design.

The Sirhowy Tram Road, built in 1802, connected the Sirhowy works to the Monmouthshire Canal, sixteen miles distant, and also continued as a double track to Newport. At Risca it spanned the Ebbw Valley on a stone bridge of 36 arches. The seal (**82**) depicts the horse-drawn trucks. 'A new horse brought excitement and speculation to the boys of Argoed and Blackwood' (*Tasker*). In 1822, a passenger service, knows as 'the Caravan', was introduced.

The Dulas Valley Railway seal (**83**) indicates well the need for engineering skill in Welsh railway construction, depicting the viaduct crossing the valley. The Vale of Llangollen Railway seal (**84**) suggests the rich inheritance of Wales: the river Dee, the limestone scarp of Mynydd Eglwyseg, and Castell Dinas Brân.

The Llanelly Railway seal (**85**) depicts horse-drawn trucks (in use 1828-35) bringing coal from the Penprys Colliery to sailing ships lying in the Loughor Estuary. The final stage in coal transport is depicted on the seal of the Barry Railway Co. (**86**) which shows the overhead loading of coal from the Rhondda into a steamship with auxiliary sails at Barry Docks, built in 1889.

84. Vale of Llangollen Railway Co.

85. Llanelly Railway and Dock Co. (1818)

86. Barry Railway Co.

Modern Urban Growth

Urban growth, stimulated in Elizabethan days by the increase in Welsh trade and industry, was to be much expanded in the Industrial Revolution. It was at this period that the large coastal towns and ports, still a feature of Wales today, developed.

Until overshadowed by the growth of Liverpool, Beaumaris was the principal port for North Wales. An established medieval borough and castle town, it had been the county town of Anglesey since the decline of Newborough (**52**). It was important in the sixteenth century for communications with Ireland, and the later post route to Holyhead passed through it *via* the ferry across the Menai Straits. In the seventeenth century, Beaumaris was important for the export of meat, butter, cheese and fish, both to the mainland and overseas. Wynne wrote (about 1620) that the citizens there had long been referred to as the 'Merchants of Beaumaris', as opposed to the 'Gentlemen of Conway'. Exports in the eighteenth century included copper ore, marble and slates.

¾ actual size

87. Beaumaris (1562)

+ *SIGILLVM·COMVNE·BVRGI+DE·BELLO MARISCO·AŌ 1562*
(The Common Seal of the Town of Beaumaris, 1562)

The Charter and privileges granted to Beaumaris by Edward I (1296) were confirmed and extended by Elizabeth I (June 22, 1562). A new common seal was engraved (**87**) showing a single-masted warship, possibly reflecting the strategic importance of Beaumaris at the time. The date *'8 Feb'* is inscribed on the hull, and at either end are displayed the two maces the borough was ordered (in 1562) to possess. This seal replaced the medieval seal, which also depicted a single-masted ship, together with an escutcheon and castle.

88. Cowbridge (1817)

THE COMMON SEAL OF COWBRIDGE

A Free Grammar School had been established in Beaumaris in 1603, a little while after the emergence of a similar school at Cowbridge. Richard de Clare had given the latter town borough status in 1254, it had a mayor from 1359, and received a new Charter in 1681. The agricultural importance of the Vale of Glamorgan was now reflected in the town's meat market, and cattle and horse fairs. Its prosperity declined in the nineteenth century, especially when it was by-passed by the South Wales Railway (1850). The town seal appropriately depicted a cow on a stone water-bridge; above are displayed the arms of the De Clares (three chevronels) and De Braose (three lions amidst crosslets.) Engraved in 1762, this seal replaced a medieval one of similar design.

89. **Cardiff** (1819)

+ *SIGILL:COMM:BAILLIV:ET BURGENS: CAERDIFF:* (The Common Seal of the Bailiffs and Burgesses of Cardiff; motto on scroll: *OPIBUS FLORENS ET NOMINE PRISCO* – 'Flourishing in wealth and in its ancient name'.)

Cardiff, now the official capital of Wales, has been from medieval times its largest town. The growth of local mining and industry, and associated trade, was to account for the spectacular increases in its population during the 19th century to 164,000 in 1900.

In the course of its long history, the city has had several different seals. The one displayed here was engraved by John Thackwell (for £10. 14. 0), following a resolution of the Court of Alderman in 1818 that 'the Common Seal be now changed.' It continued in use until the reform of local government in 1835. The arms of the de Clares, the medieval lords of Glamorgan (three chevrons) find place in the second and third quarters.

90. **Port Talbot** (1861)

+ *Common:seal:of:the:borough:of:port:talbot: restored:mdccclxi*
(inner legend: *SEEL WILLAVME SIRE DE FRISE,* The Seal of William, lord of Friesland).

The growth of Port Talbot, following the opening of the first dock in 1837, led in 1861 to the restoration of the medieval borough of Aberavon as a municipal borough under the terms of the 1835 Act.

Its seal consists of the mid-14th century seal of the 'Sire of Frise', one of the titles of Count William III or IV of Holland, which incorporates a shield with four lions rampant. Round this was added a border making it the Common Seal of the Borough of Aberavon', which was further altered to 'Port Talbot' when this new borough was created in 1921.

91. **Merthyr Tydfil** (1905)

+ *SEAL·OF·THE·MAYOR·ALDERMAN·AND BVRGESSES OF·THE·BOROVGH·OF·MERTHYR· TYDFIL*

Merthyr Tydfil sprang early to industrial importance. Assisted by local supplies of coal and ore, and by the construction of the Glamorgan Canal (1794), four ironworks had been established here by 1800, the Cyfarthfa works being the largest in Britain. In 1804, Trevithick's steam engine – the first to run on rails – made its début at Penydarren.

The seal, designed by Goscombe John after Merthyr received its new Charter in 1905, shows the martyr Tydfil who was put to death here early in the sixth century, and three discs displaying a blast furnace, Trevithick's engine, and Morlais Castle (just outside the town). The motto, taken from the writer Iolo Morgannwg, is *NID·CADARN·OND·BRODYRDDE,* 'Not Force but Fellowship.'

Administration and Social Welfare

The considerable changes in society resulting from the Agricultural and Industrial Revolutions were accompanied by a humanitarian and social awareness which gave rise, both by statute and by the charitable work of groups and individuals, to a variety of bodies concerned for public welfare.

Early Friendly Societies included 'a certain Club of Tradesmen, artists and others called the Amicable Society held at the Cross

92. Anglesey Druidical Society (1772)

NIS CWYR NAMYN DIWYD DDERWYDDON: INST.OCT.1772
(Only diligent Druids know)

The Anglesey Druidical Society, founded in 1772, consisted of an elected membership of 100 people, who met for a monthly dinner under the presidency of an Arch-druid. Their 'charitable and benevolent' objectives included rewarding bravery in saving life, making donations to hospitals and infirmaries, arranging apprenticeships for poor children, and offering prizes for agricultural improvement.

A uniform was adopted, and the seal of the Society depicted a druid's head between two oak boughs. Dwindling membership led to the winding up of the Society in 1844.

Keys Inn, Monmouth' (1787). Later such bodies included the 'Tab Dewi' Lodge (of the Order of True Ivorites) at Treorchi, and the Sir William Penn Lodge (of the Order of Oddfellows) at the Sirhowy Works: their seals are on display at the Welsh Folk Museum.

93. Neath: Poor Law Commissioners (1838)

The Poor Law Amendment Act (1834) established Boards of Guardians, based on groups or 'unions' of parishes, which were required to make provision for the relief of the poor in a workhouse or otherwise.

The Neath Union of 29 parishes, with 33 Guardians, had by 1839 built at a cost of nearly £4,000 a workhouse for 150 inmates, but it was alleged to be cold, damp and overcrowded. An infirmary was attached, to which a fever ward was added in 1851, but trained nursing staff were only employed from the 1880s. 'Cottage homes' were built for children (1877). The workhouse, used only for able-bodied paupers in its last years, closed in 1924.

The coat of arms is that of Queen Victoria.

94. Bedwellty Union Rural Sanitary Authority (1884)

The Public Health Act of 1875 constituted the Poor Law Guardians as Rural Sanitary Authorities in extra-urban areas. Their potential responsibility extended to include sewerage, water supply, refuse removal, hospital and mortuary provision, control of infection, registration of lodging-houses and the appointment of a Medical Officer of Health. They were replaced by the Rural District Councils in 1894.

95. Carmarthen Prison

Built in 1789-92 on the old Castle site to replace the squalid accommodation in the former gaol, this prison saw its last public hanging in 1829. Closed in 1922, it was later demolished (1938) to make way for the new County Hall.

96. Glamorganshire Banking Company (1836-98)

A number of small country banks, financed by prosperous cattle-drovers and wealthy industrialists, sprang up in Wales towards the end of the 18th Century. Many crashed about 1816 and 1825, but three banks, then recently founded – Williams and Rowlands, Neath, Eaton & Co. and Walters, Voss and Walters, Swansea – were amongst those which survived, and were amalgamated (1836-41) to form the Glamorganshire Banking Company. This was absorbed (1898) by the Capital and Counties Bank, which, in turn (1921) became part of Lloyds. The Company used the arms appropriated by Glamorgan, the three chevrons of de Clare.

97. Montgomeryshire County Council (1889)

SIGILLUM·COMMUNE·COMITATUS·DE·MONTGOMERY 1889
(The Common Seal of the County of Montgomery, 1889; the motto, *Powys Paradwys Cymry* (Powys, the Paradise of Wales), is a line from the poetry of Llywarch Hen.

The Local Government Act (1888) furthered the cause of social welfare by the establishment of the thirteen County Councils of Wales. The Seal for Montgomeryshire displayed a lion rampant, the arms of Prince Bleddyn of Powys (1063-73); a plough and shuttles, symbolic of the farming and textile industries of the county, complete the design.

Charities and Education

In Elizabethan times, it became fashionable to endow almshouses and grammar schools. The former were for poor men and women, (ten men and two women at Ruthin). The latter had low fees and reserved free places for poor pupils. Very often, as at Monmouth and Ruthin, almshouses and school were incorporated in the same charity, and built in close proximity. Pre-existing monastic buildings were sometimes used: the former Dominican friaries at Bangor and Brecon, and the Collegiate foundation of St. Peter at Ruthin, are examples. In the case of Brecon, the establishment involved the transfer from Abergwili of its Collegiate Church. The charities were the benefactions of local people who had made good: as Geoffrey Glyn at Bangor, Dean Goodman of St. Paul's at Ruthin, and William Jones, a London haberdasher and Hamburg merchant at Monmouth.

¾ actual size

98. Christ's College, Brecon (1541)

*(A.D.).SIG.COLLEG.CHRIST.DE.-
BRECKNOCK.FVND.
A.SER.DOM.REG.HENRIC°.OCTAV°
(1541)*
(The Seal of Christ's College, Brecon, founded by the most Serene Lord King, Henry VIII A.D. 1541).

The seal displays the Crucified Christ, the College Chapel, and the arms of the royal founder and of the See of St David's.

¾ actual size

99. Friars School, Bangor (1568)

*·SIGILLUM+LIBERAE+SCHOLAE
+GRAMMATICAE
+APUD+BANGOR*
(The Seal of the Free Grammar School at Bangor)

¾ actual size

100. Jones' Charity Monmouth (1614)

The seal of Bangor shows the master, with birch, examining two pupils wearing the tunics of their day; that of Monmouth displays the arms of William Jones: a lion rampant, with a Cornish chough as crest.

¾ actual size

101. Christ's Hospital, Ruthin (1590)

*SIGILLVM HOSPITALIS CHRISTI IN
RVTHIN 1590
ELIZABETH 32*
(The Seal of Christ's Hospital in Ruthin. 1590. 32 nd year of the reign of Elizabeth).
The seal depicts the Risen Christ, the scroll bearing the verse:
EGO SVM RESVRRECTIO ET VITA
(I am the Resurrection and the Life).

Universities

Further education in Wales during the first half of the nineteenth century was largely the domain of religious bodies, and was concerned with the training of their ministry. Amongst several early Nonconformist academies, one of great note was the Methodist College at Bala (founded in 1837) which, from 1845, published a noted literary quarterly, *Y Traethodydd.* Some years before, St David's College, Lampeter had been established (1827, by Bishop Burgess); it granted its own degrees, the B.D. (from 1852) and the B.A. (from 1865). In 1848 the National Society founded Trinity Training College for teachers at Carmarthen. The hold of the Church in education in a largely Nonconformist Wales, led men like Hugh Owen to raise funds for the creation of the non-denominational Bangor Normal Training College in 1862, and for the foundation of University College, Aberystwyth in 1872. The latter establishment owed much to chapel collections throughout Wales, and to Owen's indefatigable travelling. Further colleges followed (Cardiff, 1883, Bangor 1884), and in 1893 the University of Wales received its Charter. Swansea was founded in 1921 and Lampeter incorporated in 1971.

¾ actual size

102. St David's College, Lampeter (1830)

·sigil'·com·s·david
(The Common Seal of the College of St David)

The seal of St David's College shows the saint attired in pontifical Eucharist vestments, a book in his left hand, the pastoral staff in his right. It was designed by the College Architect, C.R. Cockerell, about 1830, in consultation with the College of Heralds (**see p.4**)

103. Cardiganshire County Council (1891)

The original buildings at Aberystwyth of the 'University by the Sea,' opened in 1872, consisted of a large hotel bought cheaply from a bankrupt firm. It is depicted on the first seal of Cardiganshire County Council, engraved about 1889. Above it the motto *Cymru Fydd* (Wales will be), and below *Goreu arf dysg* (Learning is the best weapon).

Institutions

Despite numerous obstacles, the Welsh language remained a living tongue throughout the nineteenth century. There was, at the same time, a growing appreciation of things Welsh. Already in 1751 the Society of the Cymmrodorion had been founded in London, and twenty years later followed the birth of the Society of the Gwyneddigion. Local *eisteddfodau* began to be held in 1789. The first on a national scale was held at Carmarthen in 1819, under the presidency of Bishop Burgess of St David's, with Iolo Morganwg as Archdruid. Throughout the century, notable advances were made in promoting Welsh culture and arousing national consciousness. The Cambrian Archaeological Association was founded in 1846, and in the same year Llandovery College, where Welsh was the principal language. In 1856 *Hen Wlad fy Nhadau* was composed. In 1880 the National Eisteddfod Association was formed, largely due to Hugh Owen. Six years later came the establishment of *Cymru Fydd,* the Young Wales Movement.

This climate of Welsh feeling led to the granting of Charters to the National Library and the National Museum of Wales. The former institution, established at Aberystwyth on a marine platform overlooking Cardigan Bay (on land presented by Lord Rendel), benefited from the donations of South Wales miners, from money derived from the disendowment of the Church, and from its status as a copyright Library (1911). The site of the National Museum was given by the City of Cardiff, together with the collections from its own museum. It was opened by King George V in 1927; in 1946 Lord Plymouth, by donating St. Fagan's Castle, made possible the establishment of the Welsh Folk Museum.

104. National Eisteddfod (Cardiff, 1899)

+ *Y DDRAIG GOCH A DDYRY GYCHWYN*
(The Red Dragon sets the pace)
Above: *GORSEDD Y BEIRDD* (The Gorsedd of Bards)

The seal of the Cardiff National Eisteddfod depicts a rampant dragon, taken from the city's arms. The National Museum seal bears a seated female figure holding a tablet showing the Welsh dragon. It was designed by Sir William Goscombe John, R.A. (1912), who also designed seals for Merthyr Tydfil (**91**), the Representative Body of the Church in Wales (1920) and the National Library.

105. National Museum (1912)

Disestablishment

By the nineteenth century a number of factors had made the Anglican Church a minority denomination in Wales. By 1851, three-quarters of the worshipping population were Nonconformists, and the people of Wales came to be roughly divisible into two groups: the landlords and industrial-masters, largely Anglican and Conservative; and the tenants and industrial-workers, largely Nonconformist and Liberal. Nonconformists naturally begrudged paying tithes to a Church they did not support and this led to the

¾ actual size

106. Bishop Edwards of St. Asaph (1889, **later first Archbishop of Wales (1921).**

+ *SIGILLUM ALFREDI GEORGII EDWARDS EPISCOPI ASAPHENSIS MDCCCLXXXIX*
(The Seal of Alfred George Edwards, Bishop of *St Asaph* (two keys in saltire) impaling the personal arms of bishop *Edwards* (a chevron between three fleur-de-lis).

'tithe war' of 1886-90. Towards the close of the nineteenth century the movement to disestablish the Anglican Church gained momentum. The large Parliamentary Liberal majority in 1905 paved the way for the necessary Act (1914), and after the inevitable delay caused by the Great War, the Church was disestablished, and partly disendowed, in 1920.

Amongst the natural leaders of the Anglican Church in this crisis were Bishop Alfred Edwards, a man of great ability, and Bishop Green, an expert in the Church's Constitution.

¾ actual size

107. Bishop Green of Monmouth (1921), **later second Archbishop of Wales** (1928).

THE:SEAL:OF:CHARLES:ALFRED:HOWELL:GREEN: D:D:BISHOP:OF:MONMOUTH:1921
The seal displays the arms of the see of *Monmouth* (two croziers in saltire between a besant charged with a lion and three fleur-de-lis) impaling the family arms *of Green,* (three stags trippant).

Some Periodical References

The Antiquaries Journal

vol.46 (1966), pp.104-6	G.C. Boon	*The Seal Matrix of Abergwili College, Carms.*

Archaeologia

vol.25 (1834-5), pp.619-20 Plate LXXI		*Great and Privy Seals of Owen Glyndŵr*
vol.58 (1935), pp.325-30	H.Jenkinson	'Seals for Wales' in 'The Great Seal of England''.

Archaeologia Cambrensis

vol.4 (1849), p.63	T.Wakeman	*Seal of the Corporation of Caerleon.*
vol.15 (1860), pp.281-4	R. Ready	*Catalogue of Seals connected with Wales.*
vol.44 (1889), pp.273-280, 288-292	W.de Gray Birch	*On Some MSS and Seals relating to Wales*
vol.45 (1890), pp.37-41	H. Taylor	*The Arms of Flintshire*
vol.55 (1900), pp.159-162		*The Arms of Cardiff*
vol.77 (1922), pp.383-9	W.J.Hemp	*The Town Seal of Haverfordwest*
vol.89 (1934), pp.343-5	E.A.Jones	*The Nevin Borough Silver Seal*
vol.94 (1939), pp.200-09	W.J.Hemp	*Five Welsh Seals*

The Archaeological Journal

vol.xiv (1857), pp.55-57	W.S.Walford & A.Way	*Official Seal of King Edward IV for his Chancery of Monmouth*

Journal of the British Archaeological Association

vol.12 (1856), pp.225-6 & vol.14 (1858), pp.325-6	T.J.Pettigrew	*Notes on the Seals of the Endowed Grammar Schools*
ibid. pp.56-60)	T.Wakeman	*On the Chancery of Monmouth*
vol.49 (1893), pp.1-14	A.Wyon	*Royal Judicial Seals in Wales*
vol.50 (1894), pp.66-70	A.Wyon	*Notes on Some New Seals of the King's Great Sessions of Wales*

Transactions of the Honourable Society of Cymmrodorion

vol.for 1927, pp.32-36, 54	D.L.Evans	*Some Notes on the History of the Principality of Wales (1343-76)*

Flintshire Historical Society Publications

vol.xi (1925), pp.57-68	H.Taylor	*The Arms of Flintshire*

Montgomeryshire Collections

vol.24 (1890), pp.1-10	M.C.J. + W.V.Ll.	*The Seal of Montgomeryshire County Council.*
ibid. pp.303-16	ibid	*County Council Seals of the Welsh Counties*

Transactions of the Radnorshire Society

vol.38 (1968), pp.66-7	J.M.Lewis	*Two Stone Seal-Dies from the Knighton Area*

Bulletin of the Board of Celtic Studies

vol.29, pt.III (1981), pp.531-544.	M. Siddons	*Welsh Seals in Paris*

Manuscript and Miscellaneous References

Public Record Office:	Card Index	
National Library of Wales	MS 1396E	*(Account of Thomas East, engraver, for Welsh Judicial Seals, 1687)*
ibid	MS 3854B	*(The Method of Proceeding in the Court of Great Sessions (1817),* pp.4, 17).
Cardiff Central Library	MS 3.758	(Welsh description of Owain Glyn Dŵr's Seals)
	MS 4.335	(Drawings made by B.Howlett in 1821-27 of some Welsh Ecclesiastical Seals)
	MS 4.969	(J.S. Corbett, *Seals and Arms of* Cardiff; 1906).
Carmarthen Record Office	'Autographs and Seals, Bishops of St. David's, 1718-37' (paper seals).	
Gwent Record Office	D.361.F.P.8.116	Official Seal of John Morgan, Esq., of Tredegar, Lord Lieutenant (1715)

H. Barber and H. Lewis, *The History of Friars School, Bangor* (1901) pp.128, (plate), 156.

G.G. Francis *Charters granted to Swansea* (1867), pp.143-147.

T.Matthews *Welsh Records in Paris* (1910), pp.119-121.

G.A.Taylor *Neath Borough Seals* in *Neath Corporation,* 1835-1935.

H.Turner 'Cardigan Seals and Badges,' in his *Wanderings in Cardiganshire* (1903).

Numerous individual descriptions of, or reference to, Welsh Seals, occur in the periodicals listed above and in:

W. de Gray Birch *Catalogue of Seals in the Department of Manuscripts in the British Museum* (vols.1-3, 1887-1894)

ibid *A Descriptive Catalogue of the Penrice and Margam Manuscripts* (4 ser; 1893-1905).

ibid *A History of Margam Abbey* (1897).

G.T. Clark *Cartae et Alia Munimenta quae ad Dominum de Glamorgan pertinent* (6 vols. 1910).

J. Hobson Matthews *Records of the County Borough of Cardiff* (6 vols: 1898-1911).

A.B. Tonnochy *Catalogue of British Seal-Dies in the British Museum* (1952)

A number of engravings of Welsh municipal seals, occur in:

S. Lewis *Topographical Dictionary of Wales* (2 vols; 1833).

Locations and Sources of the Seals Illustrated

BL: British Library
BM: British Museum
HCA: Hereford Cathedral Archives
NLW: National Library of Wales
NMW: National Museum of Wales
PRO: Public Record Office
UCNW: University College of North Wales
WFM: Welsh Folk Museum

1. Archives Nationales, Paris; J.392, no.27
2. NMW D.11 (on deposit from the Society of Antiquaries)
3. NMW D.21 (on deposit from British Museum: Seal Die no.858).
4. NMW Die 18.
5. BM Seal Die no.172
6. NMW Die 29.
7. NMW Die 8.
8. Town Hall, Haverfordwest.
9. NMW Die 24.
10. NLW *Penrice and Margam MS* 2046.
11. ibid. 283.
12. NMW.243
13. ibid. W.54
14. ibid. W.74
15. ibid. W.87
16. NLW. *Penrice and Margam MS.* 1973.
17. BL. *Harl.Ch.* 48 A.50.
18. Gwent Record Office D.501. 234.
19. NMW. W.286.
20. Clwyd Record Office D/PT/248
21. NMW W.291
22. ibid. 317 (from matrix in possession of Mr.E.A. Roberts of Monkton).
23. ibid. 131.
24. Gwent Record Office, D.361. E/1.118-2.
25. PRO.*E* 42/321.
26. NLW *Penrice and Margam MS* 1978.
27. ibid. 119
28. ibid. 1987.
29. ibid. 2058.
30. UCNW. *Mostyn MS.* 2167
31. Clwyd Record Office, D/NA/477.
32. NLW. *Penrice and Margam MS* 2050 (1).
33. ibid. 1973.
34. BL. *Harl.Ch.* 75 A.37.
35. HCA 2295.
36. NLW. *MC* 28(8) Wynnstay
37. NLW.*MC* 19(31) Wynnstay.
38. BL.*Cott.Ch.* XXLV, 17.
39. PRO.*DL.* 10/17.
40. NLW. *Penrice and Margam MS* 2046.
41. NMW W.4.
42. Caernarfon Record Office, XD 2/1107.
43. BL. *Harl.Ch.* 75 C.35.
44. ibid. 75 B.26.
45. ibid. 75 C.34.
46. *Archives Nationales,* J.615 (10136).
47. ibid, Roman PO 5147.
48. UCNW. *Baron Hill MS* 2149.
49. PRO *DL* 27/33
50. NMW W.205
51. NLW *Penrice and Margam MS* 2059.
52. BL Seal lxxi. 27.
53. BL Seal lxii. 19.
54. BL *Harl.Ch.* 75 C.44.
55. NMW W.236.
56. Monmouth Museum
57. HCA 1514.
58. PRO.*DL* 27/102.
59. NLW. *Penrice and Margam MS* 11.
60. BL *Harl.Ch.* 57 B.32.
61. NMW. W.123.
62. NMW. D.1.
63. BL. *Add.Ch.* 19,868.
64. PRO.*E.* 42/343.
65. NLW. *Coed Coch MS* 791.
66. HCA 1169.
67. Canterbury Cathedral, *Carta Antiqua* l.234.
68. PRO.*DL* 25/254.
69. BL.*Add.Ch.*8527.
70. BL.Harl.Ch. 75 A.48
71. Dyfed Archive Service (Carmarthen), *Lort MS* 11/554.
72. BL.*Add.Ch.*8414.
73. HCA 1775.
74. BL.*Add.Ch.*8650.
75. NLW.*MS.*1396 E.
76. PRO.*C.* 219/82.
77. PRO.*C.*219/106.
78. NCB (Llanishen) W.515.
79. ibid. 8525.
80. Gwent Record Office *D.* 591.23.31.
81. Newport Museum.
82. National Railway Museum, York. NRM 1952/79.
83. National Railway Museum, Swindon; no.18A.
84. ibid.48
85. ibid. 64.
86. ibid. 2.
87. PRO. *Wards* 2/16, 53 K/8.
88. Glamorgan Record Office, *B/Cow,* 139.
89. NMW D.38.
90. NMW W.227.
91. NMW W.212.
92. WFM D.37.
93. Glamorgan Record Office, *D.D.Gn.* 474.
94. Gwent Record Office, D.397/1525.
95. Carmarthen Museum, Abergwili.
96. Lloyds Bank, Ltd.
97. Powys County Council, Llandrindod Wells.
98. WFM D.7.
99. Powysland Museum, Welshpool.
100. Worshipful Company of Haberdashers, London.
101. Warden of Ruthin.
102. St. David's University College, Lampeter.
103. Dyfed Archive Service (Aberystwyth), Deed Package, 4/N2.
104. NMW. W.185.
105. NMW. D.45.
106. Cathedral Museum, St. Asaph.
107. WFM D.6.